Wall of Separation
The Phrase That Divided America

By Brian Godawa

"Wall of Separation: The Phrase that Divided America"
First Edition

Warrior Poet Publishing
www.warriorpoetpublishing.com

ISBN: 978-1-942858-38-6 (paperback)
ISBN: 978-1-942858-39-3 (ebook)

Dedicated to the memory of

Chief Justice Antonin Scalia

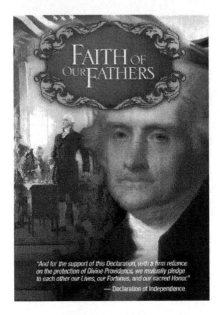

Table of Contents

Prologue

The issue of religion in politics has been a hotbed of controversy in America since its founding. And if recent history is any judge, it is not going to cool down. Most all of our presidents have been known to invoke God and religion during public speeches and in times of tragedy. Is such mixing of faith and politics a part of the American spirit? Or is it an excessive entanglement of religion and government?

In recent history, fiercely contested Supreme Court cases have addressed the issues of prayers, Bible reading, and religious instruction in public schools,[1] religious speech in public assemblies,[2] religious symbols on public property.[3] And recently, the High Court has reconsidered the constitutionality of displaying the Ten Commandments on public land.[4]

Lawsuits all across the land have sought to delete Christian symbols from city and state seals,[5] to keep creationist theories out of school classrooms, to strike "under God" from the Pledge of Allegiance.[6] In northern California, the Declaration of Independence was banned from being read in a public school because it refers to God.[7] Public school teachers and textbooks are increasingly censoring religious elements from historical events,[8] and all over the country, Christian bakers, photographers and others are being sued and arrested for maintaining biblical marriage. It seems that in America, religion and government are not on speaking terms with each other.

This cultural and institutional divide is often referred to as a " wall of separation between church and state," a metaphor deeply rooted in

1

American culture, of the belief that religion and government should not be intermixed or associated. Thus the "wall" protects both sides from contamination, ensuring a government without religious control and religion without government control.

But where does this metaphor come from? Where did it all begin?

Thomas Jefferson. Courtesy Library of Congress.

Genesis

The Setting

President Thomas Jefferson, one of the most dearly treasured Founding Fathers of this country, was both a dedicated Rationalist and a devoutly religious man who eventually became Unitarian in his faith. A strange combination to be sure. And it is Jefferson who is the one most credited with popularizing the metaphor, "wall of separation."

By 1800, just 13 years after the adoption of the United States Constitution, the country was deeply divided into its first two-party system: Federalists and Republicans. Federalists believed in strong central government and a loose interpretation of the Constitution. Republicans believed in strong state's rights and a strict interpretation of the Constitution.[9] Thomas Jefferson was a Republican. And when he ran for president against John Adams, New England Federalist clergy charged him with atheism and Deistic infidelity to the Christian faith.[10] Ironically, he was neither. He denied miracles, the deity of Christ, and the Bible as the Word of God, but he firmly believed in and prayed to a God whom he believed providentially worked in the affairs of men.[11] And like most men of his time, he considered biblical law and morality to be the foundation of good government.

Not unlike today, religion had emerged as a critical campaign issue.[12] The Federalist clergy used their pulpits to preach party politics in a way that had not been done before. It sparked a nationwide controversy and inspired in Jefferson a hatred for clergy that stayed with him for the rest of his life.[13]

Writing to his friend Benjamin Rush, Jefferson mused over how his election as president would displease the clergy...

> *And they believe that any portion of power confided to me, will be exerted in opposition to their schemes. And they believe rightly. For I have sworn upon the altar of God, eternal hostility against every form of tyranny over the mind of man.[14]*

Linking clerical religion with tyranny was a high insult in this society that had been so recently freed from the tyranny of its own despot, King George. So why did Jefferson make that kind of extreme accusation?

These politically active clergymen accused Jefferson and the Republicans of trying to separate religion from government. The accusation did not sit well with the predominantly religious populace that believed that the Christian religion was the foundation of morality and civil government.[15]

Rather than deny this belief, the Republicans scrambled to defend Jefferson's faith as Christian.[16] But they also fought back. They caricatured the preaching of ministers against Jefferson as a pursuit of the union of church and state, and created a new campaign emphasis on separating religion and politics.[17] With this strategy, the Jeffersonian Republicans used campaign rhetoric to discredit

Political cartoon attacking Jefferson.

clergy from having a voice in the public arena of debate. To these early Republicans, freedom of speech applied to everyone except their opponents.[18] And they were a success. Jefferson won the election.

The Big Cheese

On January 1, 1802, after one year in office, President Jefferson received a gift of epic proportions. With great celebration, itinerant preacher, Elder John Leland, delivered a mammoth 1200 pound Cheshire cheese directly to the President's House in Washington. It was more than thirteen feet in diameter, seventeen inches in height, took a team of six horses to carry it,[19] and was engraved with Jefferson's famous motto, "Rebellion to tyrants is obedience to God."[20] It was accompanied by an address that stated, "the greatest cheese in America, for the greatest man in America." But it wasn't an insult. It was a token of esteem.[21]

At the time, most New England states were dominated by state established churches. The Constitution had forbidden federal government from establishing religion, but not state government. The Baptists were a minority sect whose colossal gift of cheese was an expression of their gratitude and support for their Chief Magistrate's defense of religious diversity. And perhaps also a marketing gimmick for the town of Cheshire's chief manufactured product: Cheese.[22] Nevertheless, in good spirited humor, it was told the president that only milk from Republican cows was used. Federalist cows were scrupulously avoided.[23]

The Danbury Baptists

Jefferson was inspired by the occasion to respond to another petition he had recently received. The Danbury Baptist Association in Connecticut were dissenters in a state dominated by a Congregationalist establishment. The Baptists wanted freedom from the state's religious establishment. The election of Jefferson was to them a hopeful event that might influence public opinion on their behalf. And they wrote him to tell him so.

> *Our sentiments are uniformly on the side of Religious Liberty —That Religion is at all times and places a Matter between God and Individuals—That no man ought to suffer in Name, person or effects on account of his religious Opinions...Sir, we are sensible that the President of the united States, is not the national Legislator, & also sensible that the national government cannot destroy the Laws of each state; but our hopes are strong that the sentiments of our beloved President... will shine and prevail through all these States.*
>
> *– The Committee of the Danbury Baptist Association, 1801.[24]*

The Baptists were concerned that their religious liberty in Congregationalist Connecticut had devolved to the level of granted favors, rather than inalienable rights – and therefore subject to withdrawal by the state.[25] Their religious freedom was in jeopardy.

Jefferson saw in this letter an opportunity to affirm his support for dissenters of individual state churches. But there was much more to it than that. Previous presidents, George Washington and John Adams, had made it a point to proclaim fast days and thanksgiving days for the nation. Jefferson hinted in his letter that this kind of religious expression by the Chief Magistrate was reminiscent of the British monarch King George and his established national religion. And this was just the kind of excessive entanglement the founding fathers had declared their independence from.[26] Jefferson had been waiting for an opportunity to distance himself from his predecessors. And this was it. [27]

He knew his words would be published far beyond the letter's mere recipients. So he worked meticulously on revising his original draft of the letter, based on the advice and feedback of trusted administration members. He wanted this one to make an impact. [28]

The "sage from Monticello" had a reputation for using his correspondence as a means for "sowing useful truths and principles" that "might germinate and become rooted" in the American political culture. In other words, he knew his deeper political beliefs were not yet embraced by the prevailing public opinion and sought to subversively guide that opinion in his direction. [29] His language to the Danbury Baptists was calculated rhetoric.

> *Believing with you that religion is a matter which lies soley between Man & his God... I contemplate with sovereign reverence that act of the whole American people which declared that their legislature should 'make no law respecting an establishment of religion or prohibiting the free exercise thereof,' thus building a wall of separation between Church and State.*
>
> *– Thomas Jefferson, 1802.[30]*

With these words, President Jefferson, in effect, planted a Trojan Horse into the lexicon of American political discourse. It's ultimate influence on our society would not be felt for another one hundred and forty five years.

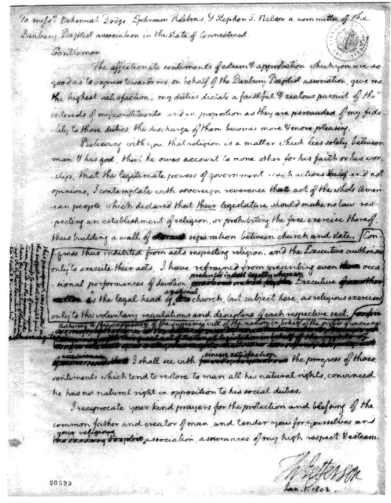

Jefferson's letter to the Danbury Baptists. Courtesy of the Library of Congress.

The Wall That Jefferson Built

But interestingly, Jefferson's own understanding of the wall of separation had little in common with the modern day interpretation. He believed the federal government could not get involved in religious matters, but that the states in fact could. Though he denied the federal Executive Branch the right to make fasting and thanksgiving proclamations, he had no reservations doing so as governor of the state of Virginia.[31] And he saw no contradiction in writing a bill enforcing the Christian Sabbath,[32] or a bill defining marriage from the Bible.[33]

That's because his notion of "separation" was a "jurisdictional" one, separating federal government and its powers on one side and state governments and denominations of churches on the other.[34]

And Jefferson's use of the word "Church" meant a separation of religious *institutions* from government, not a separation of religious *influence* from government.[35] Though he was less than orthodox in his faith, he nevertheless frequently declared God as the foundation of society's laws and government.[36] His authoring of the Declaration of Independence is his most well known text. He penned the opening words that appealed to "the Laws of Nature and of Nature's God" as the ultimate foundation and justification for U.S. political autonomy from England.

> We hold these truths to be self-evident, that all men are created equal, that they are endowed by their Creator with certain unalienable Rights.
>
> – The Declaration of Independence, July 4, 1776.

Along with Benjamin Franklin, Jefferson had proposed a picture of Pharoah's armies being destroyed at the Red Sea crossing for the Great Seal of the United States.[37]

Even after becoming President of the United States, Jefferson frequently invoked God in official addresses and public papers.[38]

And may that Infinite Power which rules the destinies of the universe, lead our councils to what is best, and give them a favorable issue for your peace and prosperity.

– Jefferson's First Inaugural Address, March 4, 1801[39]

As President, Jefferson authored the first plan of education for the city of Washington, D.C. that used the Bible as one of its principle texts for teaching reading to students.[40]

As President, Jefferson affirmed the Northwest Ordinance that encouraged religion in federal government and education.[41]

As President, Jefferson recommended multiple treaties between the federal government and various Native American tribes with the expressed intent of "promoting Christianity."[42]

As President, Jefferson not only signed bills appropriating financial support for Chaplains in Congress, but "Earnestly recommended to all officers and soldiers diligently to attend divine services."[43]

To Jefferson, national churches and state-sponsored denominations were not appropriate, but state sponsored encouragement of a generic Christianity was. His wall was a legal separation, not a moral or spiritual one.[44] Though he personally abhored established state churches, he nevertheless believed the states retained the right to make that decision for themselves.

Certainly, no power to prescribe any religious exercise or to assume authority in any religious discipline had been delegated to the General [federal] Government. It must then rest with the states.

– Thomas Jefferson, January 23, 1808.[45]

But even though Jefferson continued his religious rhetoric in political discourse, he nevertheless planted a seed of change into American politics that would germinate and take root in years to come. The seed was his "wall" metaphor that subversively reframed the religious liberty clauses of the First Amendment in terms of "separation" between Church and state. This *separation* was a departure from the *nonestablishment and free exercise of religion* as actually stated in the Amendment itself.[46]

Whereas the No Establishment and Free Exercise clauses were intended to restrict the federal government from establishing a national church and to maintain individual freedom of religion, Jefferson's "separation" expanded that idea into a division of religion and politics as entirely segregated realms of existence. It was the first brick laid in a reconceptualization of government as a secular entity without any religious influence whatsoever.

This is most likely why the recipients of Jefferson's letter, the Danbury Baptists, never acknowledged Jefferson's metaphor. Because they didn't exactly agree with it. More importantly, after the letter, no Baptist ever referred to the concept of a wall of separation in any of their official communications. Though they firmly rejected established religion, the Baptists also believed that religion had a necessary role in influencing public life *and* public policy.[47]

13

Jefferson's wall metaphor has achieved canonical status in American culture. It is more recognized than the actual text of the First Amendment.[48] Perhaps the ultimate historical irony is that Jefferson himself had no part in the actual drafting or signing of the Constitution or the Bill of Rights. He was in France at the time.

And a careful look into the debates of the first Constitutional Convention over the First Amendment reveals that not only did the Danbury Baptists disagree with Jefferson's wall metaphor, but so did the Framers of the Constitution.

Before the Wall

The Signing of the Constitution of the United States" by Howard Chandler Christy.
Courtesy Architect of the Capitol

Debate

The First Continental Congress met in 1787 to draft the Constitution of the United States of America. During the War for Independence, the states were united for battle, but poorly equipped and maintained. After the war, the economic unity between the states broke down because under the Articles of Confederation, the U.S. government had two fatal flaws: It had no power to raise money for military provisions, nor to stop trade wars between states.[49]

But the Founders wanted to protect themselves against the tyranny of centralized government, where all power is vested in one source. So they employed the concept of the separation of powers – within the branches of federal government as well as between the *federal* government and individual *states*. The Executive, Legislative and Judicial branches of the federal government were intended to operate under checks and balances. And the federal government itself would be limited only to those expressed powers specifically given to it by the Constitution. All other governmental powers not so enumerated in the Constitution were assumed by the individual states.

Thus, the limitations within the Constitution applied only to the federal government, not to the states. But this did not satisfy opponents of the Constitution. The Antifederalists, led by respected men such as Patrick Henry and Samuel Adams thought that the Constitution did not protect the states from eventually losing their authority to a centralized federal government. Though Henry was invited to Philadelphia to participate in the Constitutional convention, he did

Patrick Henry. Courtesy Library of Congress.

not go, because in his words, "I smelt a rat." [50]

> Our rights and privileges are endangered, and the sovereignty of the states will be relinquished: and cannot we plainly see, that this is actually the case? The rights of conscience, liberty of the press, all pretensions to human rights and privileges, are rendered insecure.
>
> – Patrick Henry, June 5, 1778.[51]

The Anti-Federalists wanted a Bill of Rights to secure specified liberties that the federal government could not take away. The Federalists, led by powerful communicators like Alexander Hamilton and James Madison, considered a bill of rights to be dangerous because the Constitution already restricted federal authority only to those powers granted by the Constitution.[52]

Hamilton wrote in one of his famous Federalist Papers,

> For why declare that things shall not be done which there is no power to do? I will not contend that such a provision would confer a regulating power, but it is evident that it would furnish, to men disposed to usurp, a plausible pretence for claiming that power.[53]
>
> – Alexander Hamilton, May 28, 1788.

The Anti-Federalists won the day and allowed Madison to draft the proposed Bill of Rights for debate and modification by a select committee of Congress. Each proposed Amendment was debated and rewritten multiple times before being presented to the House for debate and approval.

When discerning the purpose and intent behind the First Amendment Religious clauses, scholars often focus on James Madison, the "architect of the Constitution." In an age of great public orators, and charismatic statesmen, James Madison suffered from ill health, a weak voice and a shy disposition. But in terms of sheer intellect and determination, he was virtually unsurpassed. And it would be his leadership that would guide the drafting and debating of the Bill of Rights.[54]

Some point to Madison's united efforts with Thomas Jefferson to disestablish the state church in Virginia as the model for understanding the intent behind the Federal Amendment. But Madison's and Jefferson's view of church state separation was a minority one among the founders.

Both these men were as much influenced by Enlightenment philosophy as the Christian religion, and consequently attempted to reconcile competing truth claims of these divergent worldviews.

In Enlightenment philosophy, the supernatural authority of religion is perceived as a prejudice that blinds one from objectivity. In order to achieve a just government, the "Enlightened reasoner" believes government should remain "neutral." That is, it should be a secular state uninfluenced by the sacred. Only in this way can people be free from religious bias. In other words, government should have a non-religious bias rather than a religious bias – and all in the name of "objective neutrality."

The Enlightenment influence on Jefferson and Madison, with its secular/sacred dichotomy, was rejected by a majority of the Framers. But through Madison's deliberate leadership in drafting the Bill of Rights, the wording of the First Amendment reflected this Enlightenment separation of the secular and sacred.

Some have pointed out that the disestablishment of religion propagated by both Jefferson and Madison was really more of an establishment of the Enlightenment religion of Jefferson and Madison.[55]

But Madison was a consumate politician, well-versed in the art of compromise. And compromise he did, in order to achieve ratification of a Constitution acceptable to the majority view.[56]

On August 15, 1789, the House focused on debating the establishment clause. Earlier, Madison had tried to include language in the First Amendment that restricted State governments as well as the federal government from "violating the equal rights of conscience." Apparently, Madison actually sought to disestablish all state churches, just as he did in Virginia a year and a half earlier. But the rest of the Congress did not agree with him.[57]

James Madison. Courtesy the Library of Congress.

Representative Thomas Tucker from South Carolina moved to strike out the words about State governments and to leave the States "to themselves."[58] After multiple changes they offered up to the House another version of the Amendment .[59]

> No religion shall be established by law, nor shall the equal rights of conscience be infringed.[60]

But something was still missing. A lawyer from New York, Peter Sylvester, pointed it out. He feared that the Amendment as written, was too vague, and might eventually be interpreted to abolish religion altogether from the public square. Benjamin Huntington of Connecticut agreed. He feared that Madison's language "might be taken in such a latitude as to be extremely hurtful to the cause of religion."[61]

So Madison proposed adding the word "national" before religion, in order to clarify that the purpose of this amendment was to prohibit the federal government from establishing one sect or denomination and interfering with existing state establishments.[62]

Samuel Livermore moved that the Amendment's wording be altered to clearly establish this protection of existing state ecclesiastical arrangements. And so the new wording became:

> Congress shall make no laws touching religion, or infringing the rights of conscience.[63]

On September 3, the Senate debated their own version of the Amendment and proposed their own take:

> Congress shall make no law establishing articles of faith, or a mode of worship, or prohibiting the free exercise of religion.[64]

A conference committee from both House and Senate convened to iron out their differences and eventually settled upon the wording as we now know it.

> Congress shall make no law respecting an establishment of religion, or prohibiting the free exercise thereof.

By adding the words "*respecting* an establishment" rather than merely "establishing religion," Congress seemed to preclude federal government not only from *establishing* a religion, but also from *disestablishing* existing state churches.[65] Madison's original goal of restricting state government as well as federal government was squashed. A majority of Framers agreed that individual states had every right to establish their own churches and encourage religion among its citizens.

Also, by using the modifier "*an* establishment," rather than "*the* establishment" Congress restricted federal government only from prefering one denomination over another, while maintaining a generic preference for religion over secular government. The federal government could promote Christianity in general, but without a preference to a particular church or denomination.[66]

Religious Tests

While the U.S. Constitution does *assume* a Christian date, ("the year of our Lord one thousand seven hundred and eighty-seven"), and *implies* the Judeo-Christian Sabbath, (Article I, section 7), the only other *explicit* statement about religion, other than the First Amendment, is the prohibition of a religious test.

> No religious Test shall ever be required as a Qualification to any Office or public Trust under the United States. – Article VI, section 3.

But just what was a "religious test" to colonial Americans? Did it mean that public servants could not be discriminated against because of their religious beliefs? Did it mean *all* religions are acceptable in government, or *no* religions are acceptable?

An examination of the Constitution itself reveals that this ban on religious oaths was intended *only* for the federal government, not for state governments.

After the Preamble, the very first thing stated is that "the powers herein granted shall be vested in a *Congress of the United States*." That is, the federal government not the state governments.

In the Bill of Rights, the phrase, "Congress shall make no law" opens the First Amendment, right before the no establishment clause. This redundancy indicates a deliberate intent on the part of the drafters to prohibit only *federal* powers of establishment, not the state powers.

And just to make sure that no one would miss the point, they ended the first ten amendments with a final restatement of states' rights and powers.

> *The powers not delegated to the United States by the Constitution, nor prohibited by it to the states, are reserved to the states respectively, or to the people.*
>
> *– The 10th Amendment, the Constitution of the United States.*

Contrary to the prohibition of a religious test in federal government, the Framers considered religious tests to be entirely appropriate for state government. In fact, all thirteen states, whose governments these men represented, had their own constitutions that required or strongly encouraged the Christian faith as a prerequisite for leadership in state government.[67] The Founders would not dare to relinquish that state right.

> *No person who denies the existence of a Supreme Being shall hold any office under this constitution.*
>
> *– The South Carolina Constitution.[68]*

> *Every person who shall be chosen or appointed to any office shall subscribe the following declaration: I do profess faith in God the Father, and in Jesus Christ His only Son and in the Holy Ghost, one God.*
>
> *– The Delaware Constitution.[69]*

> *Representatives shall be chosen out of the residents in each county, and they shall be of the Protestant religion.*
>
> *– The Georgia Constitution.[70]*

> *(See Church of the Holy Trinity v. The United States for more state constitution examples)*

To the modern mind, this is almost inconceivable, but to these devout leaders, it made perfect sense. Freedom under a federal government is only maintained under the condition of localized self-government. And self-government means the right to define leadership qualifications according to community standards. And to their communities, "religion" meant general Christianity without regard to any particular sect of that faith.

Perhaps the most revealing definition of what religion meant to the Founders can be found in the original 1828 Webster's dictionary. Rather than a reference to generic spirituality, this book of contemporary word usage defined "religion" in Christian terms:

> RELIGION. Includes a belief in the being and perfections of God, in the revelation of his will to man, and in man's obligation to obey his commands, in a state of reward and punishment, and in man's accountableness to God; and also true godliness or piety of life, with the practice of all moral duties... the practice of moral duties without a belief in a divine lawgiver, and without reference to his will or commands, is not religion.[71]

Noah Webster. Courtesy Library of Congress.

So the prohibition of religious tests in the Constitution was deliberately intended by the Framers to protect the States' rights to administer their own religious tests.

In the colonial mindset, a "religious test" was more like what we would today call a "denominational test." Rather than being a generic limitation on all religious beliefs, the word "religion" in their context was a synonym for Christian faith. Though they wanted men of faith to rule, they didn't want an *established national church*, so they made sure no church's distinctives would be allowed precedence over any other. The religious test was a test for denominational distinctives, whether Anglican, Congregationalist, Presbyterian or Baptist. It was not intended to be a block against *all* religious involvement in public policy and legislation.

The Framers

To this day, some historians believe that the Founders' intentions behind the Freedom of Religion clauses and the no religious test clause were not merely to forbid a national church, but to keep religion out of government in all aspects. In other words, government should be walled off from the influence of religion.

But a simple look at the Founders' own actions at the time of the drafting of the Constitution discredits such viewpoints and establishes quite the opposite: Namely, that the Founders intended their government to not only be influenced by religion, *but to be based upon it.*

On September 25, 1787, *a mere one day* after Congress approved the First Amendment forbidding established religion, the national legislature resolved, in an overwhelming majority, to petition President George Washington to establish a national day of prayer and thanksgiving. Washington gladly accepted.

Whereas it is the duty of all nations to acknowledge the providence of Almighty God, to obey His will, to be grateful for His benefits, and humbly to implore His protection and favor, we may then unite in most humbly offering our prayers and supplications to the great Lord and Ruler of Nations; to protect and guide all sovereigns and nations, and to bless them with good governments, to promote the knowledge and practice of true religion and virtue.

-- George Washington, October 3, 1789[72]

Earlier that year, George Washington was sworn into office as the first president of the United States. He took the oath and added the words, "I swear, so help me, God." And presidents, ever since, have followed Washington's example in their inauguration ceremonies. [73]

In April, 1789, James Madison, the principle architect of the No Establishment Clause, headed up a committee to appoint and pay Congressional chaplains to open every legislative session with prayer. Church services were held in the Capitol building itself.

Even to this day, nearly all of the fifty states in the union maintain some form of prayer or devotional in their legislative meetings.[74]

At the same time that the Congress was constructing the First Amendment, they also approved the Northwest Ordinance, a piece of legislation that required all newly forming states to promote religion through various means.

Religion, morality, and knowledge, being necessary to good government and the happiness of mankind, schools and the means of education shall forever be encouraged.

– Article III, The Northwest Ordinance, July 21, 1789.[75]

And this same Congress, only years earlier, had requisitioned 20,000 Bibles to distribute throughout the nation to its citizens. And then in 1782, Congress authorized its own printing of the Bible for use in schools across the nation.[76] The presidential administrations of Washington, Jefferson, Monroe, John Quincy Adams, Jackson, and Van Buren all appropriated funds from the federal treasury to build or develop churches and their operations through treaties with Native American Indians.[77]

And the Constitution is not the only founding document of the United States. The Declaration of Independence is often referred to as having equal significance in the annals of American history. And here we read the founders appealing to "Nature's God," "the Supreme Judge of the world," as the ultimate foundation of their new nation. The text explicitly declares that men's equality and "unalienable rights" are founded upon their Creator who endows those rights to them, as opposed to the government or some other ultimate authority.

The value of religion influencing the federal government of the United States is perhaps best illustrated by a cursory look at the inscriptions and images engraved on federal monuments and government buildings.

In the Capitol building multiple works of religious art adorn its Rotunda:

1) a painting, "The Baptism of Pocahontas at Jamestown."

Detail of "Embarkation of the Pilgrims."
Courtesy of the Architect of the Capitol.

2) Another painting, "The Embarkation of the Pilgrims," where an open Bible displays the title page that reads, "The New Testament of Our Lord and Savior, Jesus Christ." The words, "God with Us" are inscribed on the sail of the ship.

3) In the House Chamber, a relief of Moses surrounded by 22 other secular *and religious* lawgivers of history.

4) In both House and Senate chambers are inscribed the words, "In God we trust"

5) On the walls of the Library of Congress: The Bible verse, Micah 6:8, He hath showed thee, O man, what is good; and what doth God require of thee, but to do justly, and to love mercy, and to walk humbly with thy God."

6) On the Liberty Bell, famous symbol of American freedom, the words of Leviticus 25:10 are prominently engraved: "Proclaim liberty throughout all the land, unto the inhabitants thereof."

The Liberty Bell

7) The Great Seal of the United States bears the Latin phrase, Annuit Coeptis, which translates to "God has smiled on our undertaking."

8) The national motto, "In God We Trust," is inscribed on all United States legal tender.

9) The Washington Monument has the Latin Words "Laus Deo," which means, "Praise be to God" engraved on its metal top.

10) The Lincoln Memorial contains the words of Lincoln's Second Inaugural Address pointing to God, the Bible, providence and the Almighty.

11) And the Jefferson Memorial bears the immortal words of the builder of the wall of separation:

God who gave us life gave us liberty. Can the liberties of a nation be secure when we have removed a conviction that these liberties are the gift of God? Indeed I tremble for my country when I reflect that God is just, that his justice cannot sleep forever.

– Thomas Jefferson, 1781.[78]

This, from the man who erected the wall of separation between church and state. How could he, and the other Founding Fathers, who fought so desperately for religious liberty, turn right around and entangle their government with the very religion they sought to disestablish?

Were they ignorant of their contradiction? Or worse, were they hypocrites, who said one thing and did another? Or maybe they never intended a wall of separation in the first place.

I have lived, Sir, a long time, and the longer I live, the more convincing proofs I see of this truth -- that God governs in the affairs of men. And if a sparrow cannot fall to the ground without his notice, is it probable that an empire can rise without his aid?

– Benjamin Franklin to the Constitutional Convention, 1787.[79]

While just government protects all in their religious rights, true religion affords to government its surest support. It is impossible to rightly govern without God and the Bible.

– George Washington, 1789.[80]

God grant that in America true religion and civil liberty may be inseparable and that the unjust attempts to destroy the one, may in the issue tend to the support and establishment of both.

– John Witherspoon, Signer of the Declaration of Independence, member of the first Continental Congress, 1802.[81]

Before any man can be considered as a member of Civil Society, he must be considered as a subject of the Governor of the Universe. Religion is the basis and foundation of government.

– James Madison, 1785.[82]

Our Constitution was made only for a moral and religious people. It is wholly inadequate to the government of any other.

– John Adams, 1776.[83]

Religion and virtue are the only foundations of all free government.

– John Adams, 1811.[84]

Of all the dispositions and habits which lead to political prosperity, religion and morality are indispensable supports. Reason and experience both forbid us to expect that national morality can prevail in exclusion of religious principle.

– George Washington's Farewell speech, written by Alexander Hamilton, 1796.[85]

A Christian Nation?

The Founders of this American nation were overwhelmingly religious. But they came from many stripes of faith. Because of this wide diversity of belief, some historians claim that when the Founders used the word, "religion," they meant a generic reference to all religions, Christian, Buddhist, Muslim, Hindu and others. But a careful look at the diversity of American beliefs in the first decades of our nation, paints a different picture. The dominant religious sects — Presbyterian, Anglican, Catholic, Unitarian, Freemason, Deism — were all denominations, heresies, or schisms of Christianity. Within the diversity of faiths, there remained a unity of a general religion. And that religion was Christianity.

The debate has raged on for decades over whether or not America was founded as a "Christian nation." Let's let the Founders speak for themselves:

[T]he Declaration of Independence first organized the social compact on the foundation of the Redeemer's mission upon earth... [and] laid the cornerstone of human government upon the first precepts of Christianity.

– John Quincy Adams, 1837.[86]

No truth is more evident to my mind than that the Christian religion must be the basis of any government intended to secure the rights and privileges of a free people.

– Noah Webster, 1828. [87]

Providence has given to our people the choice of their rulers, and it is the duty as well as the privilege and interest of our Christian nation to select and prefer Christians for their rulers.

– John Jay, the first Chief Justice of the Supreme Court, 1816.[88]

It cannot be argued too strongly or too often that this great nation was founded, not by religionists, but by Christians, not on religions, but on the gospel of Jesus Christ! For this very reason peoples of other faiths have been afforded asylum, prosperity, and freedom of worship here.

– Patrick Henry.[89]

The real object of the First Amendment was not to countenance much less advance Mohammedanism, or Judaism, or infidelity, by prostrating Christianity, but to exclude all rivalry among Christian sects [denominations] and to prevent any national ecclesiastical patronage of the national government.

– Joseph Story, United States Supreme Court Justice, 1833.[90]

From the day of the Declaration [of Independence] the people of the North American Union and of its constituent states... were an independent nation of Christians.

– John Quincy Adams, 1837.[91]

Sensible of the importance of Christian pity and virtue to the order and happiness of a state...the very existence of the republics...depend much upon the public institutions of religion.

– John Hancock, 1780.[92]

The Founding Fathers considered America a "Christian" nation. Not because every citizen was a confessing Christian, but because the government and society was based on Biblical principles as found in the Old and New Testaments. Whether Orthodox Christian, Freemason, Deist or Unitarian, they all appealed to the Bible, in differing degrees, as the ultimate standard for society and government. When referring to the idea of "religion," they had little or no thought for Islam, Buddhism, Hinduism or other non-Christian religions. These other faiths were virtually non-existent in the culture of colonial America.

To a modern American, a religious test might mean any requirement about a person's spiritual beliefs, such as "You must be a Muslim, or Christian or Jew to hold office." Or, "You must believe in God or the Bible in order to be elected." But to the Founders, a religious test would be more along the lines of a *denominational* test within Christianity: "You must be an Anglican, or a Presbyterian or a Baptist to hold office." To them, generic Christianity or the common principles of the Bible were the assumed necessary foundations of civil duty and government, and did not constitute a violation of church and state separation. It was after all a separation of *church* from state, not *religion* or *Christianity* from state.

Nearly 200 years later, the United States Supreme Court would completely deny this interpretation of "religion" and "no establishment" that the Framers had. It would turn it on its head.

> The [First] Amendment's purpose was not to strike merely at the official establishment of a single sect... It was to create a complex and permanent separation of the spheres of religious activity and civil authority.
>
> – The Supreme Court, Abington v. Schempp, 1963.[93]

What could cause such a complete revision of history, from one definition of religion to it's exact opposite? From the prohibition

32

against establishing a national church to the complete secularization of all government?

What brought Jefferson's wall of separation out of its obscure forgotten letter?

The United States Supreme Court Building

After the Wall

From the founding of the country, and for the next 150 years, the United States Supreme Court ruled decisively in favor of Christian religious values in the public sector. These were men who were either founding fathers themselves or consciously self-aware of their political heritage. The early High Court's understanding of the role of religion in the foundation of the nation and its political institutions was closely aligned with the original intent of the drafters of the Constitution. In fact, they went out of their way to establish original intent as the foundation for interpreting laws.

On every question of construction, carry ourselves back to the time when the Constitution was adopted, recollect the spirit manifested in the debates, and instead of trying what meaning may be squeezed out of the text, or invented against it, conform to the probable one in which it was passed.

– Thomas Jefferson
to Justice William Johnson, June 12, 1823.[94]

The first and fundamental rule in the interpretation of all instruments [documents] is to construe them according to the sense and the terms and the intentions of the parties.

– Joseph Story, Supreme Court Justice, 1833.[95]

Under this constitutional theory of original intent, federal *and* state Supreme Court cases in the early years of the new Republic maintained fidelity to the founders' understanding. Namely, that religion and government's interaction and support of one another did not violate the First Amendment or prohibition on religious tests.

People v. Ruggles

On September 2, 1810, in the city of New York, a man by the name of Ruggles, in the presence of other people, uttered with a loud voice the statement, "Jesus Christ was a bastard, and his mother must be a whore." He was promptly arrested for blasphemy, tried and found guilty in a New York court. He was imprisoned for three months and was ordered to pay a fine of $500 for breaking the New York blasphemy law. When he appealed, the New York Supreme Court ruled that he was guilty.

> The people of this State, in common with the people of this country, profess the general doctrines of Christianity, as the rule of their faith and practice; and to scandalize the author of these doctrines is not only impious but... is a gross violation of decency and good order.
>
> – New York Supreme Court, The People v. Ruggles, 1811.[96]

In other cases across the land, state courts upheld laws against blasphemy, profanity, pornography, sabbath breaking, and other religious laws because the Constitution did not deny state authority to regulate religious expression and therefore did not constitute religious establishment.[97] But all that was about to change.

How the Pope changed the Constitution

In 1832, a small group of clerics and intellectuals in Europe opposed the Roman Catholic union of church and state and began propagating their own version of separation. Pope Gregory XVI responded by authoring an encyclical condemning church state separation:

> Nor can we augur more consoling consequences to religion and to government from the zeal of some to separate the church from the state, and to burst the bond which unites the priesthood to the Empire.

For it is clear that this union is dreaded by the profane lovers of liberty, only because it has never failed to confer prosperity on both.[98]

Fueled by anti-Catholic fears, most Protestants in America put aside their distaste for "separation" and began to use it against Rome. By this time much of American Protestantism was deeply influenced by the Revolutionary spirit of Individualism. Many considered Roman Catholics, because of their devotion to the Pope in Rome, to be "subjects of a foreign power." To them, this papal denunciation signalled a desire on the part of Rome to seek a union of church and state in America as well. The violation of this sacred trust brought on a wave of anti-Catholic rhetoric stressing separation in order to keep Catholics from political power.[99]

But the first time that separation of church and state broke into the national consciousness was in 1840. In New York, the Public School Society had been impartially giving money to religious schools. Since they did not give preference on the basis of denomination, they did not consider this to be sectarian.

Then the Roman Catholic schools asked for some of the money. The Protestants were not happy. They began to appeal to the separation of church and state to justify keeping the Catholics from gaining access to that money. But the Catholic church pointed out that indeed, the Society *was* giving preference and being sectarian in giving money only to *Protestant* schools. To the New York Public School Society, Protestant Christianity was generic Christianity separated from state alliances, but Roman Catholicism was an "unholy alliance of church and state".[100]

New York City schools were eventually put under local district control. This decentralized the funding process but carried with it an unintended consequence. By using "separation of church and state," to exclude Roman Catholicism from public school funding, Protestants thought they were keeping their religious enemy from the public arena. But what they did not realize was that they were adding the next bricks into the wall that would ultimately separate them from the political process as well. The wall began to grow and divide the country.[101]

Dueling Amendments

The next brick in the wall of separation was laid in the decade to follow when two opposing organizations proposed amendments to the U.S. Constitution relating to the First Amendment.

Since 1863, the National Reform Association promoted a Christian Amendment that would call for a recognition of America's Christianity in the Preamble of the Constitution. By now, the new notion of "separation" had seeped deeply into the American consciousness. The attempt ultimately fizzled.[102]

But then in 1874 The National Liberal League, headed by secularist Francis Ellingwood Abbot, proposed an alternate amendment. He recognized that the Constitution did not really guarantee the separation of church and state, so he wanted to expand the First Amendment to make sure that it did. He wanted absolute separation; a secular government without religious interference.[103]

But this amendment too was ultimately overshadowed and lost in the fray of 1876 when the Blaine Amendment was proposed on the floor of the U.S. House of Representatives. Representative James G. Blaine, hoping for the Republican nomination for president, rewrote the First Amendment to restrict not only federal establishments of religion, but states rights as well. He added a clause inhibiting public funds and public lands from

James Blaine
Courtesy Library of Congress

38

ever being under control of any religious sect. It passed in the House, but failed in the Senate.[104]

The importance of these amendments lies in their social motivation. The Blaine Amendment and its genetic sibling from the National Liberal League, marked the first attempt to employ "separation" ideology to eliminate religious involvement in government. Before this, Protestants used separation to constrain Roman Catholicism, but now secularists were using separation to try to constrain *all* religious interaction with government. The wall protecting church from state transformed into a wall dividing religion from government. The wall protecting state powers from federal control was seen as a wall "protecting" state and federal government from religious influence. [105] Another brick in the wall.

But the worse was yet to come. While the effect of separationist thinking on nineteenth century American society and legislatures was certainly apparent, perhaps its clearest effects could be seen in the evolution of Constitutional interpretation of the Highest Court of the land: The Supreme Court.

United States Senate in Session. Courtesy of the Senate Curator.

The Supreme Court of the United States – Drawn by Carl J.Becker 1888. Courtesy Library of Congress

The Early Court

When the Founders drafted the Constitution and created the three branches of government, they were careful to seek a balance of power between the branches. The Legislative branch would make the law, the Judiciary would interpret the law, and the Executive would enforce it. Madison had argued that the Legislative branch was the most important in Consitutional law because it most directly represented the will of "We the people." It contained the most diversity of members, elected by regional local populations.[106]

The Courts, on the other hand, were considered the weakest and least important of the branches of government. Not only does the Constitution place the Judiciary last in order of importance, but it gives it the least amount of described powers. The Founders gave Congress the most amount of expression and description to its powers, making it the most important in terms of Constitutional law-making power.

Even the architectural designers of the national Capitol considered the Judiciary almost as a second thought, because they failed to provide it with a chamber for the Court. The first home of the Court was in a humble apartment in the basement beneath the Senate Chamber.[107]

The High Court's purpose was never to determine the constitutionality of a law, but to interpret the law passed by Congress *by applying it* to specific cases of dispute. But Madison and Jefferson suspected trouble. They were worried that if the Supreme Court decided to judge the law rather than apply it, it would end in despotic control. Making law through judicial fiat. They had seen it coming.

Refusing or not refusing to execute a law, to stamp it with its final character... makes the judiciary department paramount in fact to the legislature, which was never intended and can never be proper.

– James Madison, 1788.[108]

You seem...to consider the judges as the ultimate arbiters of all constitutional questions; a very dangerous doctrine indeed, and one which would place us under the despotism of an oligarchy... The Constitution has erected no such tribunal.

– Thomas Jefferson, 1820.[109]

Writing in *Federalist 81*, Alexander Hamilton agreed that the judicial branch would not be allowed to strike down laws passed by the legislature as unconstitutional.

In the first place, there is not a syllable in the plan under consideration which directly empowers the national courts to construe the laws according to the spirit of the Constitution.

– Alexander Hamilton.[110]

Even the early Judiciary agreed. In *Commonwealth v. Kneeland*, 1846, the High Court concluded that "no branch of government, and least of all the judiciary," had the right to interfere with the Legislature's expressed will through law.[111]

And that federal judicial respect for authority was applied to State government as well. For the first 150 years, State Supreme Courts were considered the highest authority in cases involving the Bill of Rights. The federal Supreme Court would often cite State Supreme Court decisions for it's authority, and avoided treading on that authority.

But with the growing population of Mormons in America in the early nineteenth century, free religious exercise as it related to polygamy inevitably became an important issue. Once again the High Court affirmed states rights over federal interference and stressed the nation as being a Christian one.

In *United States v. Reynolds*, 1878, *Murphy v. Ramsey*, 1885, and *Davis v. Beacon*, 1885, the Supreme Court ruled polygamy unnacceptable religious exercise because it violated Christian laws and morals. To these Courts, America was a Christian country with Christian laws, but this did not make a particular denomination of Christianity an established church.[112]

Supreme Court Justices, 1892. Courtesy Library of Congress

Holy Trinity v. United States

In 1887, The Church of the Holy Trinity in New York hired a clergyman from England to be its pastor. The United States Attorney General charged that this employment violated an earlier federal statute that made it unlawful to hire any aliens or foreigners in the United States. The Court's research exposed the fact that this law was enacted solely to stop the abusive hiring practices of railroad companies exploiting cheap labor. It reasoned that the *original intent* of laws must be considered when applying the law. The church had violated the letter of the law, but certainly not the spirit of it. It concluded that this was an "absurd" application of the law against Christianity.

> *No purpose of action against religion can be imputed to any legislation, state or national, because this is a religious people... this is a Christian nation.*
>
> *– United States Supreme Court,*
> *Church of the Holy Trinity v. United States, 1892.*

The opinion then quoted many previous state Supreme Court decisions as well as federal Supreme Court decisions, and historical evidences of colonial America to prove that America was indeed a Christian nation. And then it summarized its findings:

> These are not individual sayings, declarations of private persons: they are organic utterances; they speak the voice of the entire people...[T]he people of this country, profess the general doctrines of Christianity, as the rule of their faith and practice... We are a Christian people and the morality of the country is deeply engrafted upon Christianity, and not upon the doctrines or worship of those imposters [other religions]... These and many other matters which might be noticed, add a volume of unofficial declarations to the mass of organic utterances that this is a Christian nation.
>
> – United States Supreme Court,
> Church of the Holy Trinity v. United States, 1892.[113]

These early rulings illustrate that the judiciary branch originally perceived itself through the eyes of the Founding Fathers. It considered the country to be a religious nation, and its laws to be based on Christian principles. And that this was in no way a federal establishment of religion or a national church.

And it also understood the First Amendment restriction to apply only to federal government, while leaving state government free to regulate religious behavior.

Within a mere 55 years, all this would change. The view of the Court would become the exact opposite of how the Founding Fathers and early Courts understood the First Amendment and the relation between religion and government.

Revolution

School busing, 1940. Courtesy Library of Congress

Everson V. Board of Education[114]

In 1947, Jefferson's Trojan Horse was opened and a revolution occurred. It wasn't a violent revolution, or even a very explicit one. It was more of a subversion. It happened in the quiet chambers of the United States Supreme Court. And it was led by 5 Judges.[115]

Earlier in 1943, an Anti-Catholic activist, sympathetic with the Ku Klux Klan, filed a law suit against the state of New Jersey, for busing children to Catholic schools. His name was Arch Everson. In *Everson vs. Board of Education*, the Supreme Court used the opportunity to do something it had never done in the history of American jurisprudence. It applied the No Establishment Clause, that was intended only to restrict the federal government, *against* an individual state government. And they appealed to Jefferson's "wall" metaphor to justify it.

Neither a state nor the Federal Government can pass laws which aid one religion, aid all religions, or prefer one religion over another. – In the words of Jefferson, the clause against establishment of religion by law was intended to erect "a wall of separation between church and state."... That wall... must be kept high and impregnable. We could not approve the slightest breach.

– Supreme Court Justice Hugo Black,
Everson v. Board of Education, 1947.[116]

What the Court actually did was take the 14th Amendment, that guaranteed state citizenship rights to freed antebellum slaves, and incorporated it into the First Amendment. In *Everson*, the Court claimed that the 14th Amendment allowed it to use the First Amendment, that was intended to be a limitation on federal government, *against* state government.

Supreme Court Justices, 1940. Courtesy Library of Congress

The High Court of 1947 saw an opportunity to expand its judicial authority against state's rights of sovereignty. Rather than having only those powers delegated to it by the Constitution, the Court now became the ultimate arbiter of law – just as Thomas Jefferson and James Madison had feared.

Between 1870 and 1950, Congress had thwarted various attempts to apply the no establishment clause against the states no less than 25 times, including the infamous Blaine Amendment. But now, the Bill of Rights, originally intended to protect the states from federal intrusion, would be transformed into a weapon used against the states to revoke their authority. What Congress never intended with its legislation, the Court now achieved.[117] It was indeed a revolution, and the Supreme Court later admitted to it.

> ... And so the _revolution_ occasioned by the Fourteenth Amendment has progressed as Article after Article in the Bill of Rights has been incorporated in it and made applicable to the States.
>
> – The Supreme Court, Walz v. Tax Commission, 1970.[118]

But there was yet another twist in this courtroom drama. Even though the _Everson_ majority affirmed Jefferson's wall against the state, the final decision claimed that the state _had not, in fact, violated this separation._ Black concluded the state was not aiding religion but simply reimbursing fares paid to public school buses for children. The fact that some of them were going to religious schools was not directly connected to the State's financial involvement.[119]

The Catholics were pleased. The Separationists were screaming mad. They flooded Justice Black with criticism. But it was the perfect compromise. The perfect coup. Religious groups like the Catholics thought their interests were secure. But in reality, Black led the Court in legitimizing the wall of separation metaphor that would eventually undo _Everson_ and work toward the complete secularization of both federal and state government. In his dissent in _Everson,_ Supreme Court Justice Rutledge complained that this secularization was cloaked hostility against religion — a "complete and permanent separating of the spheres of religious activity and civil authority by comprehensively forbidding every form of public aid or support for religion."[120]

Black himself alluded to this judgment as a "Pyrrhic victory." King Pyrrhus was an ancient Greek king whose famous statement, "One more victory and I am undone" reflected the irony of winning a battle, but losing the war.[121]

Everson truly was a Pyrrhic victory: A battle won at the expense of losing the war. From this point on, Article after Article would indeed be incorporated into the 14th Amendment. But that was not the final brick in the wall of separation between church and state. Over the next 21 years the Court would completely revise history regarding the meaning of the First Amendment. And they did it through several key decisions.

McCollum v. Board of Education[122]

For 14 years after *Everson*, with the exception of *McCollum v. Board of Education* in 1948, the Court continued to rule in favor of voluntary religious activities in connection with public schooling. In *Zorach v. Clauson* (1952), Justice Douglas, writing for the majority opinion, even invoked the "wall" metaphor 13 times, while affirming that "The First Amendment does not say that in every and all respects there shall be a separation of church and state... We are a religious people whose institutions presuppose a Supreme Being."[123] But in 1962, the true consequences of *Everson* began to take hold, and one by one, the Court would seek to take away every trace of religion that existed in the public arena. The Revolution began to take root. The wall was growing tall.

Engel v. Vitale[124]

In *Engel v. Vitale*, a group of parents sued a New York school principle for maintaining a tradition of voluntary prayer in a public school. They claimed it violated their children's religious freedom. The High Court agreed. Ironically, it admitted that the prayer, a rather generic one, *did not amount to an establishment of a church*, but concluded that it nevertheless was unconstitutional.

Though the Court did not cite a single precedent for its ruling,[125] it appealed again to the "wall of separation." But it turned a new corner. *It now implied that the Founding Fathers themselves were wrong about the First Amendment.*

> New York's establishment of its Regents' prayer...seems relatively insignificant when compared to the governmental encroachments upon religion which were commonplace 200 years ago.
>
> – *The United States Supreme Court, Engel v. Vitale, 1962*[126]

In *Everson*, the Court had admitted that the Bill of Rights was not intended for the States, but applied it against them anyway. Then in *Engel*, the Court declared the original intent behind the Bill of Rights *was wrong*. A mere four years later, it would deny original intent altogether.

Abington Township v. Schempp

In 1968, the Supreme Court put the final brick in the wall that separated the First Amendment from the original intent of the Founding Fathers.

In this case, the Court ruled voluntary Bible reading in public school to be unconstitutional. Though the state of Pennsylvania maintained a policy to open classes with a student Bible reading every morning, it sought to avoid coercion and sectarianism. The student could only be a volunteer. They could choose whatever chapter and whatever Bible version they wanted. And there would be no comments before or after the reading. Children could absent themselves if they so desired. One of the children was even allowed to read from the Koran.

But this was not enough for the Court. It considered any religious activity whatsover to be inappropriate. It sought complete "neutrality" in public education. [127]

> The [First] Amendment's purpose was not to strike merely at the official establishment of a single sect... It was to create a complete and permanent separation of the spheres of religious activity and civil authority.
>
> – The Supreme Court, Abington Township v. Schempp, 1968.[128]

In a dissenting opinion, Justice Stewart unveiled the real purpose behind this language of "complete and permanent separation" used in Abington:

> A refusal to permit religious exercises thus is seen, not as the realization of state neutrality, but rather as the establishment of a religion of secularism.[129]

31 years later, in *Allegheny County v. Pittsburgh ACLU*, the High Court would admit this secularist motive. It would claim that this "neutrality" sought by the court was a mandate by the constitution "that the government remain secular."[130]

After deliberately defying the Framers' original intent for the First Amendment in *Everson*, and then declaring the Framers wrong in their intent in *Engel*, the High Court now constructed an *entirely new intent* for the Framers. That intent was a totally "secular government." And not surprisingly, it reflected the Supreme Court majority's own intent.

Walz v. Tax Commission of the City of New York

Just two years later, in *Walz v. Tax Commission of the City of New York*, the Court ruled in favor of property tax exemptions for religious institutions. And when it did, it preached the importance of seeking the original intent of the Framers, a 180 degree turnaround. But why would it do so? Because now, that original intent had been deconstructed into an entirely new creature of the Court's own creation.

[T]he line we must draw between the permissible and the impermissible is one which accords with history and faithfully reflects the understanding of the Founding Fathers.

– Justice William Brennan, Walz v. Tax Commission of the City of New York, 1970.[131]

[O]ne of the mandates of the First Amendment is to promote a viable pluralistic society and to keep government neutral, not only between sects, but also between believers and unbelievers.

– Supreme Court Justice William Douglas Walz v. Tax Commission of the City of New York, 1970.

Though the *Walz* case upheld tax exemptions for religious bodies, such as churches, Justice Burger and others grew concerned that a rigid application of the First Amendment would ultimately cause a clash of the two Religion clauses. In the relentless pursuit of a separationist interpretation, "free exercise" would soon be prohibited in the name of "no establishment." Burger had seen it coming.[132]

The revolution had come of age. The coup was complete. The wall was built and reinforced with a new history. But is this pluralism of beliefs and "secular" government neutrality really what the Founders intended? Did they really want the Bible and prayers removed from public education? Did they really avoid public encouragement of religion?

It is impossible to rightly govern without God and the Bible.

– George Washington, 1789.[133]

History will also afford frequent opportunities of showing the necessity of a public religion... and the excellency of the Christian religion above all others, ancient or modern.

– Benjamin Franklin, 1749.[134]

[O]nly one adequate plan has ever appeared in the world, and that is the Christian dispensation.

– John Jay, First Chief-Justice of the U.S. Supreme Court.[135]

At the time of adoption of the Constitution, and of the [First] Amendment... the general, if not the universal sentiment in America was, that Christianity ought to receive encouragement from the State...An attempt to level all religions, and to make it a matter of state policy to hold all in utter indifference would have created universal disapprobation, if not universal indignation.

– Joseph Story, United States Supreme Court Justice, 1840.[136]

The magistrate ought to encourage piety...[and] make it an object of public esteem. Those who are vested with civil authority ought... to promote religion and good morals among all under their government.

– John Witherspoon, signer of the Declaration of Independence, 1815.[137]

Tests for Establishment

By 1970, the Supreme Court had fully reversed its interpretation of the First Amendment from the original intent of the Founders, into a new paradigm of mandated secularization of the public square. In the next 20 years, new cases would produce a series of tests that would help the High Court legislate which laws were and which were not an establishment of religion within this new paradigm. The wall of separation was now being reinforced with barbed wire, lest any religion try to creep in through the cracks.

The Lemon Test

In 1971, in *Lemon v. Kurtzman*, the Court struck down two different state statutes from Rhode Island and Pennsylvania that secured payment for substitute public schoolteachers hired from religious schools. Though these teachers were not teaching religion in the public school setting, their mere presence was forbidden simply because of their own school's religious nature.

The Court created what is now called, "The Lemon Test" In order to filter out such religious presence in the public schools. It says that a state statute is constitutional if it meets three criteria: "First, the statute must have a secular legislative purpose; second, its principal or primary effect must be one that neither advances nor inhibits religion, finally, the statute must not foster "an excessive government entanglement with religion."[138]

The Endorsement Test

In 1985, in *Wallace v. Jaffree*, the Court struck down a statute that allowed for one-minute of silence in Alabama public schools. Justice O'Connor stressed what she called the "Endorsement Test" evident in their concerns. Namely that since the originator of the law claimed he did not have a secular purpose to the law, but merely a religious one for prayer in school, then the law could be construed to be an endorsement of religion that is unconstitutional.

Yet another change in the evolving meaning of church state separation. Now, the First Amendment concept of no *establishment* of religion had morphed into no *endorsement* of religion.

But this decision and its other related rulings were not without dissent – aggressive scholarly dissent. Chief Justice Warren Burger called the attack on the Alabama statute bordering on, if not trespassing into the ridiculous.[139] He maintained the ruling did not manifest "neutrality, but hostility toward religion."[140] And he concluded with acerbic wit, "The mountains have labored and brought forth a mouse."[141]

In another dissent, Justice William Rehnquist penned one of the most memorable sieges against the wall of separation and it's stranglehold on the American consciousness.

There is simply no historical foundation for the proposition that the Framers intended to build a "wall of separation" that was constitutionalized in Everson...But the greatest injury of the "wall" notion is its mischievous diversion of judges from the actual intentions of the drafters of the Bill of Rights...The wall of separation between church and State" is a metaphor based on bad history... It should be frankly and explicitly abandoned...Our perception has been clouded not by the Constitution but by the mists of an unnecessary metaphor.

– Justice William Rehnquist, dissent in Wallace v. Jaffree, 1985.[142]

Separationism reigned as the dominant paradigm, but not without a good fight.

The Psychological Coercion Test

In 1992, in *Lee v. Weisman*, the latest test would be constructed by the Court. It would be called the "psychological coercion test." At issue was public invocations or prayers at school graduation ceremonies. The Court concluded that a rabbi praying a generic prayer and asking everyone to stand constituted "psychological coercion" on the individual student whose father filed the lawsuit. [143]

This new test established that if anyone becomes uncomfortable around a religious practice in public, that practice is unconstitutional.

The dissenting opinion, led by Justice Scalia, pointed out that the Majority decision was again, as in *Engel v. Vitale*, "conspicuously bereft of any reference to history."[144] The Court had concluded somehow that allowing a rabbi to pray at a school ceremony was the equivalent activity of government engaging in religious practices.[145] Just how a public school has become federal government itself was not explained.

By Their Fruits You Shall Know Them

With some exceptions,[146] the Lemon Test, the Endorsement Test and the Psychological Coercion Test, would be used by the Court to declare most religious involvement in the public arena as unconstitutional.

In *Committee of Public Education v. Nyquist* (1973), the Court forbade the City of New York from reimbursing private schools for building repair and maintenance as well as reimbursing poor families for private school tuition.

In *Luetkemeier v. Kaufmann* (1973), the Court upheld the restriction of transportation reimbursement to private religious schools, contrary to its original decision in *Everson*.[147]

In multiple cases like *Wheeler v. Barrera* (1974), [148] New York v. Cathedral Academy (1977),[149] and *Aguilar v. Fenton* (1983),[150] the Court restricted public aid to private religious schools, regardless of its negative effect on the poor and disadvantaged.

In *Edwards v. Aguillard* (1987) the Court forbade a Lousiana law mandating equal time to teach creation science in the classroom along with evolution.[151]

In *Texas Monthly, Inc. v. Bullock* (1988), the Court forbade tax exemption for religious publications.[152]

In *Allegheny v. ACLU* (1989), the Court forbade a nativity scene from being displayed in a Pennsylvania County Courthouse.[153]

In *Santa Fe v. Jane Doe* (2000), the Court forbade students at public high schools from freely praying at football games.[154]

Over the years, the separationist paradigm as embodied in the Lemon test, endorsement test and psychological coercion test has been challenged, altered and even weakened in its hold on the Supreme Court.

In a 2002 decision supporting school vouchers for private religious school tuition, Justice Clarence Thomas seriously questioned the separationist consequences of the *Everson* decision and even suggested a return to the original intent of the Framers.

> [W]hile the Federal Government may "make no law respecting an establishment of religion," the States may pass laws that include or touch on religious matters so long as these laws do not impede free exercise rights...There would be a tragic irony in converting the Fourteenth Amendment's guarantee of individual liberty into a prohibition on the exercise of educational choice.
>
> – Justice Thomas, *Zelman v. Simons-Harris.*[155]

In a series of other cases between 1981 and 2001, the Court actually affirmed the right of student religious groups to access public school facilities.[156] This schizophrenic contradiction of rulings demonstrates that the secular/sacred dichotomy may be dominant in the Supreme Court, but it is not absolute in its control over all the justices. The wall of separation between church and state was being scaled both from without *and* within.

Moses and the Ten Commandments mural in the Pennsylvania Supreme Court.
Courtesy of American Vision.

A Higher Law

O
f all the First Amendment cases related to the wall of separation between church and state, perhaps none are as important as those that have dealt with the Ten Commandments. Every wall has a foundation. Without it, that construction will fall and crumble. By examining and making judgments regarding the Ten Commandments in public venues, the Court is addressing the very foundations of its own legal authority.

Ever since the dawn of history, man has followed systems of law in order to maintain order in society. The Code of Hammurabi, the Ten Commandments of Moses, the Constitution of the United States. Behind every system of law, whether ancient or modern, is a god. The "god" is the source of the law, the ultimate authority that determines justice. If the source of the law is the individual, the individual is the god of the system. If the source of the law is the Court, the Court is the god of the system.[157]

The Framers of our Constitution knew this well. They knew that if they did not base their law on a higher authority, then whoever was in power would determine what the law said. Whoever was in power would become the god of the system. They called this "tyranny."

To avoid tyranny, they sought to found their Constitutional Republic upon a higher law. That higher law was the Ten Commandments of the Bible.

We have staked the whole future of American civilization... upon the capacity of each and all of us to govern ourselves... according to the Ten Commandments of God.

– *James Madison.*[158]

The moral principles and precepts contained in the Scriptures ought to form the basis of all our civil constitutions and laws.

– *Noah Webster, 1832.*[159]

The sanctions of religion compose the foundations of good government; and the ethics, doctrines, and examples furnished by Christianity exhibit the best models for the laws.

– *Dewitt Clinton, United States Senator, 1823.*[160]

Rather than maintaining the Founders' original intent behind the foundation of law, the Supreme Court has increasingly undermined it, establishing itself as the ultimate arbiter of constitutional questions. Just as Jefferson had warned.[161]

The Constitution...is a mere thing of wax in the hands of the judiciary, which they may twist and shape into any form they please.

– *Thomas Jefferson, 1819.*[162]

Chief Justice Charles Evans Hughes confirmed Jefferson's fear when he said in 1930, "We are under a Constitution. But the Constitution is what the judges say it is."[163] This godlike pronouncement from the bench of the Supreme Court can only be achieved through the philosophical and political replacement of the Supreme Being with the Supreme Court. And the way to achieve that coup is to dethrone that Supreme Being's foundation for law: The Ten Commandments.

Scales of Justice in the Supreme Court. Courtesy of the Supreme Court

Stone v. Graham

In 1980, the Supreme Court struck down a Kentucky statute requiring the posting of the Ten Commandments in public school classrooms. In an attempt to meet the Lemon Test demand for secular purpose, the Kentucky legislature required a notation at the bottom of each posting. It read, "[t]he secular application of the Ten Commandments is clearly seen in its adoption as the fundamental legal code of Western Civilization and the Common Law of the United States."

In a move unprecedented in the history of Establishment Clause cases, the High Court made a summary judgment without a hearing. The majority opinion utterly disregarded the Commandments' secular purpose as the foundation of Western law. It concluded that the sacred nature of some of the Commandments invalidated that secular purpose. To the Justices' horror, such displays may actually "induce schoolchildren to read," and perhaps even "to venerate and obey, the Commandments." [164]

Justice Rehnquist dissented. In the face of this anti-religious hysteria, he warned about the impossibility of trying to eliminate all reference to religion in the public sector:

The Establishment Clause does not require that the public sector be insulated from all things which may have a religious significance or origin. This Court has recognized that "religion has been closely identified with our history and government," and that "[t]he history of man is inseparable from the history of religion,"

– Justice Rehnquist, Stone v. Graham.[165]

Even with such cutting logic, Rehnquist also missed the real irony. It was not merely that the Ten Commandments are part of the secular history of America, but that they are the very foundation of the legal system upon which the Supreme Court rules. In effect, the judges were dismantling the basis of their own authority. An authority that the Founding Fathers acknowledged with thorough devotion.

The general principles on which the fathers achieved independence were… the general principles of Christianity.

– John Adams to Thomas Jefferson, 1813.[166]

[C]an the liberties of a nation be thought secure when we have removed their only firm basis, a conviction in the minds of the people that these liberties are of the gift of God? That they are not to be violated but with His wrath? Indeed, I tremble for my country when I reflect that God is just; that his justice cannot sleep forever.

– Thomas Jefferson, 1794.[167]

Religion and morality...are the foundations of all governments. Without these restraints, no free government could long exist.

– Pennsylvania Supreme Court, 1824.[168]

Apocalypse Now

In *City of Elkhart v. William Boos* (2001) the Court refused to consider an appeal regarding a lower court decision to remove a monument of the Ten Commandments from an Indiana municipal building.[169]

Again, in November, 2003, the Supreme Court refused to review another controversial Ten Commandments case, *Moore v. Glassroth*. Alabama Chief Justice Roy Moore had refused to obey a federal court order to remove a 2.6 ton monument of the Ten Commandments from an Alabama courthouse. The Justice was removed from his office for "willfully and publicly" defying the order. [170]

But Moore had appealed to the Constitution as his higher authority. He claimed that the act of a federal judge declaring that the state cannot acknowledge God is itself defiance against both the United States Consitution and the Alabama state constitution which require acknowledgment of God. It was not Judge Moore who was acting above the law, it was the federal court judge who ordered the removal.[171]

But Moore went even further. He said that it would be illegal for the state to prohibit the acknowledgment of God in the Ten Commandments because they are the very foundation of the U.S. legal system. The wall of separation between church and state, in this sense, was an illegal wall, built upon a false foundation.[172] This case created a firestorm of controversy from major evangelical and atheist organizations around the country.

But the High Court could not put this issue off for very long. It was too pressing. So it announced it would hear two cases involving displays of the Ten Commandments on government property in March of 2005 in *ACLU v. McCreary* and *Van Orden v. Perry*.[173]

The High Court ruled in *Van Orden* that Ten Commandments displays do not violate the Establishment Clause if they are "passive" markers for the historical influence of religion on government. By *passive*, they meant that citizens are not required to observe them in a confrontational manner. They may just as easily walk by as to stop and notice.

> From at least 1789, there has been an unbroken history of official acknowledgment by all three branches of government of religion's role in American life...Texas' display of the Commandments on government property is typical of such acknowledgments. Representations of the Commandments appear throughout this Court and its grounds, as well as the Nation's Capital. Moreover, the Court's opinions, like its building, have recognized the role the Decalogue plays in America's heritage...While the Commandments are religious, they have an undeniable historical meaning. Simply having religious content or promoting a message consistent with a religious doctrine does not run afoul of the Establishment Clause.
>
> – The Supreme Court, Van Orden Vs. Perry.[174]

Because of the difficulty in trying to balance a separation of church and state with an equal avoidance of "hostility to religion," (the so-called "neutrality" doctrine) the majority, led by Chief Justice Rehnquist, concluded that the usual standard for discerning establishment violations, the Lemon Test, was not applicable. The Ten Commandments are, after all, equally religious *and* historical in their significance. Justice Breyer actually exempted the case from *all previous* Establishment tests as well.[175] In the Court's eyes, this recognition and display of the Ten Commandments is not an establishment of religion, but a mere "passive" recognition of the historical influence of religion on government.

Yet, in a shocking contradiction, this same Court simultaneously ruled in *McCreary County* that Ten Commandments displays are unconstitutional if their primary purpose is to communicate historical influence of religion on government. The defendants in the case displayed the Ten Commandments in a Kentucky courthouse, along with other historical documents in a collection entitled, "The Foundations of American Law and Government Display." The other documents were the Magna Carta, the Declaration of Independence, the Bill of Rights, the lyrics of the Star Spangled Banner, the Mayflower Compact, the National Motto, the Preamble to the Kentucky Constitution, and a picture of Lady Justice.

Each document had an explanation of its legal and historical importance. The display of the Ten Commandments contained the following:

> The Ten Commandments have profoundly influenced the formation of Western legal thought and the formation of our country. That influence is clearly seen in the Declaration of Independence, which declared that 'We hold these truths to be self-evident, that all men are created equal, that they are endowed by their Creator with certain unalienable Rights, that among these are Life, Liberty, and the pursuit of Happiness.' The Ten Commandments provide the moral background of the Declaration of Independence and the foundation of our legal tradition.[176]

In essence, this new majority, led by Justice Souter, interpreted the *purpose* behind these displays to be religiously motivated, regardless of the "secular" truth of their influence on American history and legal tradition. So contrary to *Van Orden*, religious and secular influence on history is *not* a legitimate validation for displaying American historical documents if the personal beliefs of the presenters are somehow omnisciently determined to have religious motives. Certain religious observations and conclusions about America's history and foundations are simply not allowed by the thought police of the High Court liberal contingent. A bizarre ruling that reflects the fact that this majority is not the same majority as *Van Orden*.

In his delivery of the majority opinion in *Van Orden*, Chief Justice Rhenquist catalogued various examples of federal buildings in the very Capitol that recognize the role the Decalogue has played in America's heritage. He noted...

Not only is there a relief of Moses in the United States House chamber -- amidst other secular and religious lawgivers...

...but in the Library of Congress, there is a large statue of Moses holding the Ten Commandments, alongside a statue of the Apostle Paul...

And in the Department of Justice, a statue including the Ten Commandments inside...

As well as a medallion depicting the Ten Commandments on the floor of the National Archives...

Moses in the Library of Congress. Courtesy Library of Congress

But most ironic of all are the many sculpted depictions of Moses or the Ten Commandments -- on and in the Supreme Court building itself.

On the South Courtroom frieze of the Chamber, over the Justices heads...

...On the stone carvings of the East Pediment...

...Engraved on the large oak doors of the Chamber...

...On the support frame of the Courtroom's bronze gate,

67

...And twice in the Great Hall metopes.

In light of this ubiquitously acknowledged historical *and* religious foundation of the Ten Commandments, the Supreme Court has run into an impregnable wall of a problem. By declaring religious "purpose" behind public displays of the Ten Commandments unconstitutional, the Court, in effect, has declared its own practices and history to be unconstitutional. It has declared the founding and framing of our country to be unconstitutional. Worse, it has declared its own *authority*, based on the Law of God itself, to be unconstitutional.

How long can the Supreme Court suffer the contradiction of its own rulings? How long can a nation endure when it removes the very foundation of its entire justice system? For when the foundation for law is removed, a transcendent standard is replaced by arbitrary power. The rule of law is replaced with the rule of brute force. Democracy is replaced by tyranny.

Those who will not be governed by God will be ruled by tyrants.

– William Penn, Founding Father. [177]

George Washington Praying. Courtesy Library of Congress.

The Future of this Great Republic

So America stands at a crossroads. A wall of separation between church and state has been built upon the faulty foundation of a secular government without religious influence. A metaphor created by a single Founding Father has so dominated the American political landscape that it has obscured the real meaning of the First Amendment it was supposed to illuminate. Though the Framers wrote the Bill of Rights to protect state government from the encroachment of federal government, the Supreme Court has turned those federal Amendments into a weapon against the states. Though the First Amendment religion clauses were intended to avoid a national church denomination, they have been reshaped into a guarantee of a national religion of secularism. Though the Founding Fathers created a government founded upon and influenced by the Christian religion, separationists have sought to rewrite that history and divorce government from all religious influence whatsoever.

Brick by brick, Supreme Court Decision by Supreme Court decision, our country has built a wall that our Founding Fathers fought so hard to avoid. A wall prohibiting the free exercise of religion in the name of "no establishment." A wall where the very religion that formed the basis of American political theory, is fast becoming the one religion unnacceptable in the public square.

There have been many more cases in the new millennium regarding church state relations. Some, like *Obergefell vs. Hodges 2015*, have serious ramifications on religious freedom. But the die has been cast.

The next step will be the suppression of Christian faith in both the public and private spheres of citizens. The *Obergefell* decision virtually institutionalized gay marriage, and is already being used to define homosexuality as a civil right. The logical conclusion of such legal manipulation is to force all Christians to embrace sexual perversion as morally acceptable or suffer the consequences of complete legal, social and economic destruction. Christian bakers, photographers, and other creative services that refuse to participate in the celebration of gay marriage are under legal assault.

The next step will be to force Christian ministers to marry homosexual couples or lose their churches. After all, if homosexuality is a civil right, then the opposition to it must be bigotry, and if your religion condemns it, then that religion will be dehumanized into a religion of bigotry, hatred and intolerance. To these moral monsters, Christians who support biblical marriage are the same as racists who lynched blacks under Jim Crow. The end game of this is clear: the justification of violence against Christians. After all, if Christians are just like lynchers of yesteryear, then it must be all right to destroy them legally, economically, socially and even physically.

The persecution is already beginning. We need a new generation of spiritual warriors who will not withdraw from government, but participate in it to bring reform and righteousness, "to do right; to seek justice; to defend the oppressed" (Isaiah 1:17). One organization that you can support does just that with amazing effectiveness in the courts, including the Supreme Court. It is called Alliance Defending Freedom (adflegal.org), and I recommend you begin by letting them educate you on the issues and then support them financially. I gain no personal or financial benefits from this recommendation. I merely support them for their righteousness.

We can bring change, but we must get involved to protect our brothers and sisters, or we will be ruled by tyrants.

About the Author

 Brian Godawa is the screenwriter for the award-winning feature film, *To End All Wars*, starring Kiefer Sutherland. It was awarded the Commander in Chief Medal of Service, Honor and Pride by the Veterans of Foreign Wars, won the first Heartland Film Festival by storm, and showcased the Cannes Film Festival Cinema for Peace.

He previously adapted to film the best-selling supernatural thriller novel *The Visitation* by author Frank Peretti for Ralph Winter (*X-Men, Wolverine*), and wrote and directed *Wall of Separation*, a PBS documentary, and *Lines That Divide*, a documentary on stem cell research.

Mr. Godawa's scripts have won multiple awards in respected screenplay competitions, and his articles on movies and philosophy have been published around the world. He has traveled around the United States teaching on movies, worldviews, and culture to colleges, churches and community groups.

His popular book *Hollywood Worldviews: Watching Films with Wisdom and Discernment* (InterVarsity Press) is used as a textbook in schools around the country. In the Top 10 of Biblical Fiction on Amazon, his first novel series, *Chronicles of the Nephilim*, is an imaginative retelling of Biblical stories of the Nephilim giants, the secret plan of the fallen Watchers, and the War of the Seed of the Serpent with the Seed of Eve. The sequel series, *Chronicles of the Apocalypse*, tells the story of the apostle John's book of Revelation, and *Chronicles of the Watchers* recounts true history through the Watcher paradigm.

Find out more about his other books, lecture tapes and DVDs for sale at his website, **www.godawa.com**.

Get More of the Wildest Christian Imagination Out There

Chronicles of the Nephilim

Chronicles of the Apocalypse

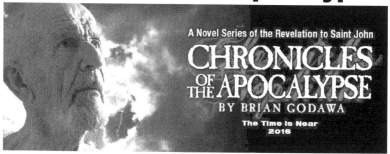

A Novel Series About the Book of Revelation & the End Times. A Fresh Biblical View.

www.Godawa.com

   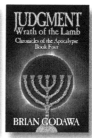

Chronicles of the Watchers

A Series About the Watchers in History.
Action, Romance, Gods, Monsters & Men.
The first novel is *The Dragon King: First Emperor of China*

www.Godawa.com

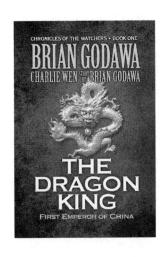

End Notes

[1] Engel v. Vitale, 370 U.S. 421 (1962), Abington School District v. Schempp, 374 U.S. 203 (1963), McCollum v. Board of Education, 333 U.S. 203 (1948).

[2] Santa Fe Independent School District v. Doe, 530 U.S. 290 (2000)

[3] County of Allegheny v. American Civil Liberties Union, Greater Pittsburgh Chapter, 492 U.S. 573 (1989)

[4] "Commandments cases get hearing before high court: Justices to revisit church-state separation," The Associated Press, Updated: 8:07 p.m. ET Oct. 12, 2004 (http://www.msnbc.msn.com/id/6232020/), Stone v. Graham, 449 U.S. 39 (1980)

[5] IN THE UNITED STATES DISTRICT COURT FOR THE WESTERN DISTRICT OF MISSOURI SOUTHERN DIVISION, Case No. 98-3306-CV-S-RGC, B. JEAN WEBB, Plaintiff v. CITY OF REPUBLIC, MISSOURI, Defendant
http://www.law.umkc.edu/faculty/projects/ftrials/conlaw/republiccomplaint.html;
"ACLU wants cross rubbed out of L.A. County seal" By The Associated Press, 05.27.04
<http://www.firstamendmentcenter.org/news.aspx?id=13425>

[6] "Court dismisses Pledge case: Atheist father cannot sue over use of 'Under God'" Tuesday, June 15, 2004 Posted: 5:22 PM EDT (2122 GMT), cnn.com <http://www.cnn.com/2004/LAW/06/14/scotus.pledge/>

[7] "Declaration of Independence Banned at Calif School" Wed Nov 24, 2004 04:12 PM ET, By Dan Whitcomb. LOS ANGELES (Reuters)
<http://www.reuters.com/printerFriendlyPopup.jhtml?type=topNews&storyID=6911883>

[8] "Schools, God and Thanksgiving" Steve Chapman, Chicago Tribune online, November 25, 2004
<http://www.chicagotribune.com/news/columnists/chi-0411250169nov25,1,4516182.column>

[9] "United States Federalist Party" From Wikipedia
<http://en.wikipedia.org/wiki/United_States_Federalist_Party>

[10] Daniel Dreisbach, *Thomas Jefferson*, p. 29. Philip Hamburger, *Separation*, p. 113.

[11] Eidsmoe, Christianity and the Constitution, pp. 215-246.

[12] Dreisbach, *Thomas Jefferson*, p. 18

[13] Dreisbach, *Thomas Jefferson*, p. 28-29; Hamburger, *Separation*, p. 147.

[14] Andrew Lipscomb and Albert Ellery Bergh, *The Writings of Thomas Jefferson*, 20 vols 10:175; Dreisbach, *Thomas Jefferson*, p. 28.

[15] Hamburger, *Separation*, p. 117.

[16] Hamburger, *Separation*, p. 117-120. Eidsmoe, *Christianity and the Constitution*, p. 216.

[17] Hamburger, *Separation*, p. 112.

[18] Dreisbach, *Thomas Jefferson*, p. 29.

[19] Dreisbach, *Thomas Jefferson*, p. 12.

[20] Dreisbach, *Thomas Jefferson*, p. 9-10.

[21] Dreisbach, *Thomas Jefferson*, p. 13.

[22] Dreisbach, *Thomas Jefferson*, p. 10.

[23] Hamburger, *Separation*, p. 156; Dreisbach, *Thomas Jefferson*, p. 10.

[24] Hamburger, *Separation*, p. 158.

[25] Dreisbach, *Thomas Jefferson*, pp. 31-33.

[26] Dreisbach, *Thomas Jefferson*, p. 39.

[27] Dreisbach, *Thomas Jefferson*, p. 21.

[28] Dreisbach, *Thomas Jefferson*, p. 34.

[29] Dreisbach, *Thomas Jefferson*, p. 44.

[30] Dreisbach, *Thomas Jefferson*, p. 17

[31] Dreisbach, *Thomas Jefferson*, p. 59, 68.

[32] DeMar, America's Christian Heritage, p. 65;

[33] Dreisbach, *Real Threat*, p. 121-22.

[34] Dreisbach, *Thomas Jefferson*, p. 51ff; *Real Threat*, pp. 114,115,124.

[35] Dreisbach, *Thomas Jefferson*, p. 51, 55-56.

[36] Daniel Dreisbach, Mark D. Hall, Jeffrey H. Morrison, *The Founders*, p. 57-67.

[37] Gary DeMar, America's Christian Heritage, p. 66; Dreisbach, Founders on God, p. 73.

[38] Dreisbach, *Thomas Jefferson*, p. 58; Federer, *America's God*, p. 327.

[39] Dreisbach, *Thomas Jefferson*, p. 57; quoting Jefferson, First Inaugural Address, 4 March 1801, *Writings of Jefferson*, 3:320, 323.

[40] William J. Federer, *America's God*, p. 324.

[41] Federer, *America's God*, p. 325-26; David Barton, *The Myth of Separation*, p. 37-38.

[42] Dreisbach, *Real Threat*, pp. 127-128.

[43] Federer, *America's God*, p. 328; Dreisbach, *Real Threat*, p. 130.

[44] DeMar, America's Christian Heritage, p. 67; Dreisbach, Real Threat, p. 123.

[45] Barton, *Original Intent*, p. 19; Dreisbach, *Real Threat*, pp. 114-115, 126.

[46] Dreisbach, *Thomas Jefferson*, p. 51-54.

[47] Dreisbach, Thomas Jefferson, p. 51-53.

[48] Dreisbach, *Thomas Jefferson*, p. 3.

[49] DeMar, *God and Government*, p. 141.

[50] DeMar, *God and Government*, p. 159.

[51] Ketcham, Anti-Federalist Papers, p. 199

[52] Dreisbach, *Real Threat*, p. 55-58.

[53] Dreisbach, *Real Threat*, p. 55-56; *The Federalist Papers*, No. 84, p. 437.

[54] Dreisbach, *Real Threat*, p. 136.

[55] Dreisbach, *Real Threat*, p. 107.

[56] Dreisbach, *Real Threat*, pp. 105-111.

[57] Dreisbach, *Real Threat*, p. 58.

[58] Dreisbach, *Real Threat*, p. 62-63.

[59] Dreisbach, *Real Threat*, p. 58.

[60] Dreisbach, *Real Threat*, p. 59.

[61] Dreisbach, *Real Threat*, p. 60.

[62] Dreisbach, *Real Threat*, p. 61.

[63] Dreisbach, *Real Threat*, p. 61.

[64] Dreisbach, *Real Threat*, p. 64.

[65] Dreisbach, *Real Threat*, p. 65.

[66] Dreisbach, *Real Threat*, p. 65.

[67] DeMar, *America's Heritage*, pp. 23-30.

[68] DeMar, America's Heritage, p. 28.

[69] DeMar, *America's Heritage*, p. 23; Federer, *America's God*, p. 203.

[70] DeMar, America's Heritage, p. 25.

[71] Barton, *Myth*, p. 30.

[72] Federer, *America's God*, p. 654; Dreisbach, *Real Threat*, p. 66-67.

[73] DeMar, *America's Heritage*, p. 52-53.

[74] DeMar, America's Heritage, p. 52.

[75] Barton, *Myth*, p. 38.

[76] Barton, *Myth*, p. 104-106.

[77] Dreisbach, *Real Threat*, p. 129.

[78] DeMar, America's Christian Heritage, p. 58-59.

[79] Barton, *Myth*, p. 109.

[80] Barton, *Myth*, p. 113; Ferderer, *America's God*, p. 660.

[81] Barton, *Myth*, p. 117.

[82] Barton, *Myth*, p. 120; Federer, *America's God*, p. 410.

[83] Barton, *Myth*, p. 123.

[84] Barton, *Myth*, p. 123.

[85] Barton, *Myth*, p. 124.

[86] Barton, *Original Intent*, p. 158-159.

[87] Barton, *Myth*, p. 126: Federer, *America's God*, p. 677.

[88] Barton, *Myth*, p. 78.

[89] Barton, *Myth*, p. 25; Federer, *America's God*, p. 289.

[90] Federer, *America's God*, p. 575.

[91] Barton, *Original Intent*, p. 163

[92] Barton, *Original Intent*, p. 171.

[93] Barton, *Myth*, p. 150.

[94] Federer, *America's God*, p. 330-331.

[95] Joseph Story, Commentaries on the Constitution of the United States, Vol. III, pp. 383-400 (1833).

[96] Barton, *Myth*, p. 57.

[97] Barton, *Myth*, pp. 51, 55, 58.

[98] Hamburger, *Separation*, p. 230-231.

[99] Hamburger, *Separation*, p. 230.

[100] Hamburger, *Separation*, p. 222.

[101] Hamburger, *Separation*, p. 228.

[102] Hamburger, *Separation*, p. 290-293.

[103] Hamburger, *Separation*, p. 289-290, 293.

[104] Hamburger, *Separation*, p. 297-298.

[105] Hamburger, *Separation*, p. 302.

[106] Barton, *Myth*, 225.

[107] Barton, *Myth*, 222.

[108] Barton, *Myth*, 223.

[109] Barton, *Myth*, 223.

[110] Barton, *Myth*, 224.

[111] Barton, *Myth*, 225.

[112] Barton, *Myth*, 67-72.

[113] Barton, *Myth*, p. 50.

[114] Hamburger, *Separation*, p.454+; Dreisbach, *Jefferson*, p. 100+; Barton, Myth, p.

[115] Dreisbach, *Thomas Jefferson*, p. 100.

[116] Hamburger, *Separation*, p. 461.

[117] Dreisbach, *Real Threat*, p. 92, 95; Barton, *Myth*, p. 169-170.

[118] Barton, *Myth*, p. 168-169.

[119] Hamburger, *Separation*, p. 469.

[120] Dreisbach, *Real Threat*, p. 150.

[121] Hamburger, *Separation*, p. 462.

[122] Hamburger, *Separation*, p. 472+; Barton, *Original Intent*, p. 145+;

[123] Dreisbach, *Real Threat*, p. 125; Hitchcock, *Supreme Court vol. I*, p. 92.

[124] Barton, *Original Intent*, p. 149+' *Myth*, p. 145+; Dreisbach, *Thomas Jefferson*, p. 102+

[125] Barton, *Original Intent*, p. 152.

[126] Barton, *Myth*, p. 147. *Engel v. Vitale*. In a later year (1983), Justice Brennan would suggest that the Founding Fathers were simply mistaken in their authorization of religious practices like appointing chaplains. Hitchcock, *Supreme Court vol. I*, p. 109.

[127] Barton, *Original Intent*, p. 154-155.

[128] Dreisbach, *Real Threat*, p. 113; Barton, *Original Intent*, p. 158.

[129] Barton, *Original Intent*, p. 156.

[130] Barton, *Original Intent*, p. 175.

[131] Barton, *Original Intent*, p.160.

[132] Hitchcock, *Supreme Court vol. I*, p. 119-120.

[133] Barton, *Myth*, p. 113; Ferderer, *America's God*, p. 660.

[134] Barton, *Original Intent*, p.162.

[135] Barton, *Original Intent*, p.162.

[136] Federer, *America's God*, p. 574.

[137] Barton, *Original Intent*, p.171.

[138] *Lemon v. Kurtzman* decision.
<http://caselaw.lp.findlaw.com/scripts/getcase.pl?court=US&vol=403&invol=602>

[139] Barton, *Original Intent*, p. 172.

[140] Barton, *Original Intent*, p. 172.

[141] Hitchcock, *Supreme Court vol. 1*, p. 103.

[142] Barton, *Original Intent*, p. 173.

[143] Barton, *Original Intent*, p. 177+;

[144] Barton, *Original Intent*, p. 180.

[145] Barton, *Original Intent*, p. 178.

[146] Sex Ed, Sodomy law, Hitchcock, *Supreme Court vol. 1*, p. 117-118; Nativity crèche and paid chaplains Hitchcock, *Supreme Court vol. 1*, p. 108-109; *Tilton v. Richardson*, Hitchcock, *Supreme Court vol. 1*, p. 126; *Mitchell v. Helms* (financial aid) Hitchcock, *Supreme Court vol. 1*, p. 145.

[147] Hitchcock, *Supreme Court vol. 1*, p. 131.

[148] Hitchcock, *Supreme Court vol. 1*, p. 131.

[149] Hitchcock, *Supreme Court vol. 1*, p. 135.

[150] Hitchcock, *Supreme Court vol. 1*, p. 137.

[151] Hitchcock, *Supreme Court vol. 1*, p. 107.

[152] Hitchcock, *Supreme Court vol. 1*, p. 121.

[153] Hitchcock, *Supreme Court vol. 1*, p. 110-11.

[154] Hitchcock, *Supreme Court vol. 1*, p. 105.

[155] ZELMAN, SUPERINTENDENT OF PUBLIC INSTRUCTION OF OHIO, et al. v. SIMMONS-HARRIS et al. Justice Thomas Concurring.
<http://caselaw.lp.findlaw.com/scripts/getcase.pl?court=US&vol=000&invol=00-1751>See Hitchcock, *Supreme Court vol. 1*, p. 148.

[156] Widmar (1981), Mergens (1984), Lanb's Chapel (1993), Rosenberger (1995), Good News (2001). See Hitchcock, *Supreme Court vol. 1*, p.161.

[157] John Eidsmoe, Christianity and the Constitution, 1987, p. 409.

[158] Barton, *Myth*, p. 120.

[159] Barton, *Myth*, p. 125; Federer, *America's God*, p. 678.

[160] THE LIFE AND WRITINGS OF DEWITT CLINTON, WILLIAM W. CAMPBELL. Transcribed by Bill Carr. <http://www.history.rochester.edu/canal/bib/campbell/Chap09.html>

[161] Barton, *Myth*, p. 223.

[162] Barton, *Myth*, p. 236.

[163] Barton, *Myth*, p. 233.

[164] STONE v. GRAHAM, 449 U.S. 39 (1980) <http://caselaw.lp.findlaw.com/cgi-bin/getcase.pl?navby=volpage&court=us&vol=449&page=41>

[165] STONE v. GRAHAM, 449 U.S. 39 (1980) <http://caselaw.lp.findlaw.com/cgi-bin/getcase.pl?navby=volpage&court=us&vol=449&page=41>

[166] Barton, *Original Intent*, p. 26.

[167] Barton, *Myth*, p. 246.

[168] Barton, *Myth*, p. 248.

[169] Hitchcock, *Supreme Court vol. 1*, p. 116.

[170] CNN.com. "Ten Commandments judge removed from office" Friday, November 14, 2003.
<http://www.cnn.com/2003/LAW/11/13/moore.tencommandments/>; "Judge suspended over Ten Commandments: Ethics complaint: Chief justice failed to respect, obey law" Saturday, August 23, 2003 <http://www.cnn.com/2003/LAW/08/22/ten.commandments/>

[171] "Alabama chief justice: 'Judges can't make the law'" CNN.COM, Tuesday, September 2, 2003 Posted: 10:55 PM EDT (0255 GMT) <http://www.cnn.com/2003/LAW/09/02/cnna.moore/>

[172] "Alabama chief justice: 'Judges can't make the law'" CNN.COM, Tuesday, September 2, 2003 Posted: 10:55 PM EDT (0255 GMT) <http://www.cnn.com/2003/LAW/09/02/cnna.moore/>

[173] "Justices Agree To Hear 2 Cases On Display of Commandments" By Charles Lane, Washington Post, Wednesday, October 13, 2004; Page A03 <http://www.washingtonpost.com/wp-dyn/articles/A26439-2004Oct12.html>

[174] http://caselaw.lp.findlaw.com/cgi-bin/getcase.pl?court=US&navby=case&vol=000&invol=03-1500. Justice Rehnquist, majority opinion.

[175] *ibid.*, Justice Breyer, concurring.

[176] *Ibid.*, Justice Souter, majority opinion.

[177] Federer, *America's God*, p. 500.